Junkshopping with Sari

By Sari Kaysser

PUBLISHED IN ASSOCIATION WITH
This Week MAGAZINE

Publishers **GROSSET & DUNLAP** *New York*

I would like to thank the following for their help and encouragement in preparing this book: Russ Hunt; Bruce Troyer, Absolute Photos; Mrs. Marci Braun, Director of Programming, WFLD-TV; Mrs. Alice Milner (my mom); the Wagon Wheel Trading Post, Lisle, Illinois; and Treasure and Trinkets, Downer's Grove, Illinois.

Contents

No, this is not my antique sleigh blanket, but a "nearly new" mink stole from a thrift shop which became an attractive skiing hood. These can also be turned into pillows and accessories for your wardrobe.

1.

For the Love of Junk!

THOUGH I call myself a "junkshopper," I don't look like a junk woman (well . . . occasionally, perhaps). But in my heart there's nothing I like better than rummaging thru grandma's attic or attending garage sales, rummage sales, flea markets, auctions, antique shops, trading posts or anything where I can find an inexpensive little white elephant, and turn it into . . . something.

Here's how I became a "junkie" in the first place. Five years ago, my husband and I bought our first home in a suburb on the outskirts of Chicago. Prior to that, we'd rented a furnished apartment. We didn't have *any* furniture. And our only accessories were the man and woman from our wedding cake, and our wedding album.

My husband, Don, said, "We're not going to charge a houseful of furniture like most couples do. We're going to buy our furnishings with cash. Piece by piece, as we can afford it."

(I guess we've all heard that one. Right, girls?)

I could just see us ten years from then, still trying to fill that big empty house. So, I asked him if he'd let me bring home something, just anything, from a shop I'd seen in town—Grandma's Attic.

Reluctantly, he agreed. And handed me a five-dollar bill. (Isn't he generous?)

Now, I'd never been in an antique shop, and when I stepped into Grandma's Attic, I was absolutely thrilled. Hundreds of fascinating treasures were strewn ceiling to floor, shrouded in shadows, dust and cobwebs. And I noticed this odor. . . .

(I've noticed this same musty odor in all antique shops. In fact, once you get addicted to it, your car won't drive by without automatically turning in. At least that's what I keep telling my husband.)

There were no price tags on the items, because it wasn't fashionable to be a junkshopper six years ago. You could still get a bargain.

Over in a dark corner of that shop I saw just what I'd always wanted—a black bearskin rug! The proprietor said I could have it for five dollars.

"Four seventy-five," I trilled. And that was the first bargain of my "junkshopping" career.

I'll never forget that crisp autumn day, and how thrilled I was as I shoved that old rug into my car and headed home to show Don. It was a beautiful day, and the wind ruffled the black fur . . . well, maybe it was a little orange with age, but it *was* a genuine bearskin.

I raced up the front stairs calling, "Don. Don! Wait till you see what I've got for our bedroom!"

He took one look. Clearly, I'd committed a "nono" in his eyes.

So I showed him an ad from a popular decorating magazine. I'm sure you've seen this ad or one like it. It's of a beautiful fireplace, with a white bearskin rug in front and a lush masterbed beside it. Well, hubby reminded me, we didn't have a fireplace, and we were sleeping on a cot.

"We have to start someplace," I suggested.

So we dragged the rug in and spread it on the bedroom floor. Immediately, the whole house smelled like wet skunk. It could only be the rug. I hadn't noticed it in the shop. (Let's face it, the shop had its own deodorant problem.) And driving home with the windows down . . . Well, we couldn't live with it, so I took it to an expert furrier.

He took one look, stepped back, and said, "Mrs. Kaysser, that 'thing' is not a rug!"

I too stepped back. What was it? Was it alive!

"Step into it," he ordered, from a safe distance.

Fearfully, I unzipped one end, stepped into the rug and pulled it up around my shoulders.

Can you guess what it was? A sleeping bag? No. But you're close. It was a genuine antique sleigh blanket! A real antique! And I'd got it my first time out in the shops. But it still stunk . . . and the furrier said he couldn't to a *thing* about it.

Well, I wasn't going to be defeated. I brought that old bear home and threw it in a bathtub of cold water. Into this, I poured a whole can of detergent. I slopped the stinky thing up and down, dragged it thru the house, dripping and odorifering, and threw it over our patio fence to dry.

Two weeks later, when it was finally dry, I got the vacuum out to try to fluff up all that matted fur. I fluffed and fluffed and pretty soon I had . . . a nice leather board with about two hairs on it!

Believe me, I was discouraged. My first attempt at "junkshopping" was a complete flop. But I didn't give up. I kept trying, and I found that each time I went into the shops, my imagination got better. I could find more uses for more "junk." When I started writing articles about my "junkshopping" experiences, I wrote what has become a famous (in my circles) quote on this subject. It's sure to touch your heart: "Imagination is like sterling silver, the more you use it, the brighter it gets."

Isn't that lovely? Well, it may be a little corny, but it's true!

✽✽✽✽✽✽✽✽✽✽✽✽✽✽✽✽✽✽✽✽✽✽✽✽✽

And remember . . . when in a junk shop, the gal who hesitates is lost. So go ahead and do it.

My children (left to right), Terra, Troy and Tamma. Troy is holding the false teeth molds described in the next chapter.

2.

Who's Nuts!

I'VE always preached "imagination" to my three children. Finally, my five-year-old son, Troy, who is probably the most uncreative child I've ever met, asked if he could make a decoration for his bedroom.

Flabbergasted, I said, "Anything, Troy. Anything at all!"

He took an old water bucket, filled it with acorns and set it on his bedroom dresser. Five days later, his whole bedroom was filled with little white worms. . . .

A denmother told me what to do about this. Bring your nuts in and put them in a potato chip can. Add a handful of mothballs, cover, and let sit for a month. Dip the nuts in regular floor wax, one by one, and they're preserved for life. (Isn't that what you've always wanted to know?)

Well this *is* the kind of hobby that you have to sink your teeth into. You have to be willing to experiment a little. And don't worry, if you should loose your teeth in the process, you can always get a new set in the junkshop. And they only cost about fifty cents.

I couldn't resist getting these old false teeth molds for Don on Father's Day. He has a marvelous imagination—

he turned them into an ashtray for his den. It's a funny thing, but we can't seem to keep our "smoking" friends for long.

Terra, our seven-year-old daughter, has a very active imagination, according to her second grade teacher. About a month ago, she proved it to us.

"Mom," her fresh little face sparkled. "Why don't you let Dad bring those teeth into the kitchen. Then he won't have to get his hands cold when he takes the cubes from the icetrays?"

✷✷✷✷✷✷✷✷✷✷✷✷✷✷✷✷✷✷✷✷✷✷✷✷

Fellow junkshoppers often wail and moan that they *must* give up this habit because their homes are literally "filled with junk." I always ask what they've done in the children's bedrooms. Usually, it's not too much. The junkshopper, if she's badly addicted (and most of us "junkies" are) is relieved to have discovered a new outlet for her creative energies. For a little while longer, she can put off the black day when she must either open a shop and go professional, or have a massive, heart-breaking garage sale, or move into a larger home, or (heaven forbid) go off "junking."

One of the first kiddie items I picked up was an old school desk. You've all seen them, I'm sure, but have you ever seen a miniature, nursery school desk? I hadn't. And, I loved it. Weathering in the yard of an antique shop, it was literally on its last leg. I got it for three dollars.

Terra claimed it as soon as she saw it.

"Let me fix it up for studying. It'll look darling in our room."

I was delighted because this would be the first project Terra had ever done alone.

Shortly after that, I heard a horrible shriek from the garage where Terra was hosing-down the desk. I charged down and started shrieking, too. A whole army of tiny black spiders was swarming from the desk. I turned the hose full on them, but they kept coming. We ran into the

Terra at her antique, nursery school desk.

house and slammed the door. Later, armed with a can
of bug spray, we crept out. The spiders had disappeared!
As Terra painted the desk with yellow enamel, and the
iron legs with barn red, I stood guard with my trusty
broom. But the spiders have never appeared again. I mean,
I've never *seen* them in the garage. Hopefully, little black
spiders just fade away. . . .

I "planted" a vase of flower-tipped pens and pencils in
the tiny inkwell on the desk. Terra uses these every night
when she does her homework. She needed a study lamp,

too, so I bought a kerosene lamp and electrified it with a kit that costs a dollar in most lamp shops. (You just screw the socket on any small container or bottle.)

The drapes in the girls' bedroom have a bright red, orange and green circus animal design. I copied this, with tempera paints, on a glass lamp chimney. Try hand-painting your own glass lampshades. Remember, tempera paints wash off if you make a mistake.

Most kerosene lamps have a glass bottom where the kerosene used to go. I filled this with colorful gumdrops. You know, it's fun to have something that no one else in the whole world has. . . .

If that school desk is Terra's favorite thing (and it is), the shadow-box puppet theatre is Tamma's. She can sit for hours manipulating my antique dolls thru the stories she makes up.

This puppet theatre is a very good idea, one that you might want to copy. Find an old shadow box and gently remove the back. Spray paint it and string a curtain across the back with wire and thumbtacks. Make a "set" with miniature furniture, books, dishes, plants or whatever you and your offspring can come up with.

My curtain is an antique lace scarf. The "set" is hand-carved wooden furniture from the junkshop, naturally.

For puppets, use old Barbie dolls, stocking puppets or anything else. I use 100-year-old porcelain dolls that I painstakingly restored with glue, straight pins and paint.

To operate the theatre, throw a sheet over a chair. Your child can kneel behind it and work the dolls without the audience seeing her. Kids love it. Needless to say, it's a constructive way to keep them busy.

At birthday parties, the puppet theatre is really a hit. Let each child make his own puppet from a brown paper bag with construction paper eyes, nose and mouth. Give each a turn "backstage," while you serve popcorn and announce the "acts."

When not in use, the shadow box hangs on the bedroom wall as part of a grouping of "girl-oriented" objects from

Tamma with her shadow-box puppet theatre.

junk shops. Here, a horse's bit, painted pink, dangles long, colorful hair ribbons. (It's the only way to keep them neat.) An old slate hangs from a velvet ribbon. Terra's profile, cut in black paper, nestles on lace in a gilt frame. And a child's "bedtime" prayer is hammered on an antique brass plaque.

Usually not more than a dollar (unless they're made of real brass), birdcages make adorable accessories for a girl's bedroom, too. When my children were babies, I created a mobile from a small birdcage. I sprayed it pink, decorated it with artificial flowers, and hung plastic birds inside on rubber bands. I sprayed a scrap of light-weight dogchain to match, and attached one end to the top of the cage. I'm a very untalented carpenter, so I'll never know how I got a wall-type, arm bracket nailed securely to the ceiling. Anyway, I bet you've already figured it out—I attached the other end of the chain to this arm, and the cage dangled right over the crib. When baby pushes the cage, the birds jiggle, and he giggles! This makes a darling shower gift, too.

13

Tamma's birdcage, now a bathroom decoration.

When Tamma outgrew her crib, I hung the cage in a dreary corner of the bathroom. Stuffed full of pink flowers, it perks up the whole room.

Troy's room sports a pair of old waterskis that I painted bright blue. With molly screws, I attached squares of pegboard to one wall. (If anyone walked into that room with a large magnet, the whole wall would come tumbling down.) Using pegboard brackets, I mounted the skis so they can be used as shelves. Pull the foot supports apart and they become bookends. The rest of the shelf displays a model ship that Troy picked out in an antique shop, his autographed baseball, shells, an old ship lantern and other of his treasures.

I spray-painted a real canvas life preserver, then oil-painted boats and his name on it. He's proud that it says "Captain Troy." Life preservers also make wonderful picture or mirror frames.

His room, obviously, has a nautical theme. We added to this effect, Troy and I, when we decorated a regular window shade with bright nautical flags. We painted these

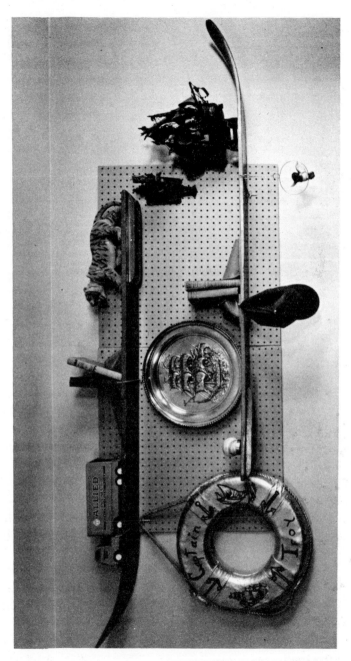

Troy's waterski wall.

Marci Braun, of WFLD-TV, and I on set for "Sari the Junk-shopper," inspecting Troy's stuffed-animals ship.

on, and added stripes, polka dots, and so on with colored tape.

Lastly, for a special Christmas gift, I made him a huge ship to hold all the stuffed animals kids have. I found this beautiful four-foot-long hull on Chicago's Maxwell Street. It was pine wood and I knew it would be handsome when refinished. For sails, I used fiberglass materials. As I'd hoped, the oil paints stiffened the material. The colorful sails (supposedly reflecting the setting sun) brighten up and help balance the wall opposite his waterskis.

✳✳✳✳✳✳✳✳✳✳✳✳✳✳✳✳✳✳✳✳✳✳✳✳

If you don't apply a little imagination to your junk . . . that's what it will be!

3.

Sock It to Dad!

HAS your husband ever made disparaging remarks about some of your antique "finds"? It seems to be a fairly common complaint. Though I find more and more men are joining us, and they're usually very, very clever when they do. Well, if your husband hasn't joined us yet, why don't you bring home something specially designed to please him.

Wouldn't he love a hanger made of two horseshoes welded together to make a hook? To make this, purchase two horseshoes for about a dollar. If they're very rusty, soak them in a solution of equal parts vinegar and water overnight. Scrub lightly with steel wool and rinse under cool water. When dry, spray with flat black paint. (See page 85.)

There are two things that every woman needs in her lifetime—a soldering iron and a motorcycle. Right? So, girls, get yourself a children's soldering iron kit in the toy department of your local department store and either solder the horseshoes together (or have them welded) so that one is flat, the other curving out to form a hook.

One of the two things that every woman needs—a motorcycle.

I asked Don what he'd do with this fine creation. He said he'd hang it on the bathroom wall and hang the toilet tissue on it. . . . Didn't I tell you he has a marvelous imagination?

Actually, these horseshoe hangers are charming when hung on the kitchen wall to hold tea towels. And many of the students in my "junk artistry" classes at the "Y" have used them as tie racks. But, again, Don came up with the best idea: he hung two horseshoe hooks on the den wall, and laid his shotgun across them. It makes a perfect gunrack!

(At Christmas, when I was looking for a gunrack for

my brother, I noticed that most racks are made to hold a single-barreled gun. So all you girls with double-barreled shotguns . . . horseshoe hangers are the answer!)

✠✠✠✠✠✠✠✠✠✠✠✠✠✠✠✠✠✠✠✠✠✠✠

There's lots of ways to get your man interested in "junking." But Tom Sawyer had the best idea. While whitewashing Aunt Polly's fence, he acted like he was having a ball. Soon all the nieghborhood kids wanted to try their hand at it. That's just what I did one evening while working on an old wooden plaque.

I'd purchased this artifact for a quarter. A label on the back registered it with an art gallery, but the picture on the front had all but faded away. Armed with brushes and oils, I smiled and hummed as I tried to recreate the pround ship that had originally sailed this picture.

The "Tom Sawyer Effect." My husband, Don, and Troy discover the joys of junking.

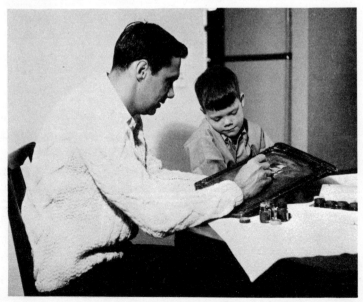

Don's masterpiece.

Soon Don was hungrily looking over my shoulder. Astounded (because he'd never painted anything but the house), I asked if he'd like to try his hand at it. He nearly pushed me out of my chair as he took over. And he created a masterpiece. I call it that because it's attractive, with artful shading and a good feel. Often people ask who the artist was when they come into our home for the first time. Don isn't *too* proud. Ha!

✸✸✸✸✸✸✸✸✸✸✸✸✸✸✸✸✸✸✸✸✸✸

And here's a "camp" little idea that dad might like. Get an old hi-button shoe. (Did you know that today these are selling for about ten dollars? And it was only two or three years ago that people were throwing them out.) I've heard many uses for these charming antiques, but Don suggested that I slide a pilsner-style beer glass down into the shoe and, naturally, fill it with beer for our next guest.

I've seen the shoes filled with cement and used as doorstops or bookends, but my own favorite idea is to slide a glass baby bottle down into the shoe, spray it with plastic preservative, and fill it with your favorite bouquet of fresh, dried or permanent flowers. It makes an adorable accessory for your bedroom dresser or an end table. Could anything so attractive be so simple? It is.

My "campy" shoe.

And while we're talking about antique clothing . . . I guess you've all heard about the thrift shops in New York, the ones that Barbra Streisand used to visit. Well I had the opportunity to visit these shops while making a TV appearance there a while ago. Other tourists would visit the Empire State Building, and so on, but I spent every minute in the shops off Broadway. These are even more interesting than junkshops. They're filled with old theatrical clothes and make-up.

It was in one of these—Stagedoor I think it was called—that I chanced to find a small beaded bag. It was black, covered with rusty beads and sporting a black chain and locket. I doubted that it was much of a "find." Anyway, I paid a dollar and brought it back to Chicago with me.

Shortly after this I was reading in a large Chicago newspaper a column about the fashions in Paris. Imagine how delighted I was to discover that the debutants in Paris were actually fighting over little antique purses. Apparently, they're the "in" thing to carry when you go to the discotheque to frug or bugaloo. In fact, according to that article, the shops couldn't even keep them in stock.

I wanted to learn to frug, so I hauled that old purse out and scrubbed those rusty beads with silver polish. And beneath the rust? Real metal beads! Now I suspected I had chanced to get a treasure. I held my magnet against the chain; it was repelled. This meant it was brass, silver, copper or gold. I rubbed the polish on the handle, chain and locket. It was sterling silver. When Don came home from work that night, I asked him to take me out, anywhere, where we could dance.

Don and I had a ball that evening. As a matter of fact, we saw the proprietor walking toward us and we were certain he was going to put us in one of those "go-go cages" to demonstrate. But guess what? He turned out to be the curator of antiques for that hotel, and he wanted to examine my purse. In fifteen minutes, he was back.

"Congratulations," he smiled. "Mrs. Kaysser, you're the proud owner of a lovely "chastity purse."

My "chastity" purse.

Isn't that delightful! I mean, wouldn't you have been thrilled? . . . Well, he wanted to buy it because, he said, it was a museum piece, It was meant to hang at the waist by that locket.

Naturally I told him I couldn't sell it.

"It just suits my personality," I told him.

He suggested that I take a look inside the purse. "The lining," he cooed, "is a sow's ear."

Well, you've all heard the saying that "you can't turn a sow's ear into a silk purse." But did you know that you *can* turn it into a beaded bag?

❈❈❈❈❈❈❈❈❈❈❈❈❈❈❈❈❈❈❈❈❈❈

You're never too old and it's never too late to start junking. So do it tomorrow.

4.

Little Things Mean a Lot

IDEAS are free for the making. And once you're tuned-in to creating something out of nothing, you'll agree that junkshopping is terrific.

When you first start wandering through the shops, play a game with yourself. Try to see how many things you'd turn into something else. Don't take it too seriously, though, or you'll turn your imagination off. Imagination is one thing that can't be pushed. Let it flow, easy, relaxed. Just a game.

Once, while playing this game in a shop in Chicago's Old Town, I chanced to see a wooden box filled with rusty old barrel keys. I knew that barrel keys weren't made anymore, at least not in volume. And I'd seen them selling for fifty cents apiece and up in the shops in the suburbs. My imagination started whispering that antique keys, when cleaned-up and painted, would make adorable earrings, tie clips, necklaces, pins, buttons and shoe buckles.

I still don't know how I mustered the courage to offer the dealer fifty dollars for the whole box full of keys. I do

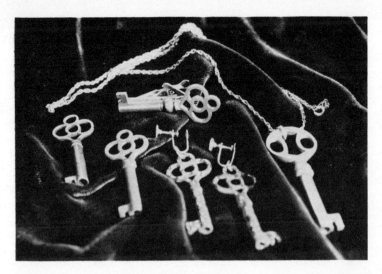

Some of my keys after a little soaking in vinegar and water.

know that that's the most money I've ever spent in a junkshop. I remember carrying that heavy load to the car, and the sudden sinking feeling that I'd just been stuck with a lemon.

Don's face when he saw that box of about 600 rusty old keys told me that he thought I belonged in a cell, the kind without a key. And frankly, I was beginning to agree with him because the rust wouldn't scrub off the keys.

Desperate, I called our local pharmacist and asked if he knew of any chemical that would remove rust from metal. (And some of these keys were even welded together with rust.) He suggested that I soak the keys in equal parts vinegar and water in a plastic container.

Bless his heart, he saved the day!

After two days of soaking, each key needed just a little scrub with steel wool and it was ready for painting. I used a rust preventative base coat. In my spare moments, I still haul out several keys and hand-paint them with hobby enamels. Color and design are dictated by my mood. Mostly, they're mod.

Many of the smaller keys can become earrings when attached to earring backings from the hobby shop. (Twelve cents a pair.) To do this, I use tiny jewelers' pliers or Epoxy.

In the beginning, when I had enough key jewelry to make up a sales kit, I ordered professional jewelry boxes lined with cotton. One thing more was needed—a name. Every product has to have a label, so why not "Sari's Junkeys"?

Labels, I discovered, are expensive to have made. So I ordered address labels for fifty cents with "Sari's Junkeys" instead of my address printed on them. When glued on the boxes, they looked very professional. Now I was ready to make sales calls on all the boutiques in the area.

To my amazement, some shops wanted to carry necklaces and tie clips, while others only wanted the earrings and pins. Before the end of the day, everything was placed, a price was agreed upon, and I only had to wait for the dollars to roll in. So I thought.

I waited and waited for that first sale. Often, I called the boutiques to see how things were going. They weren't. Discouraged, I all but gave up. Then, a five dollar check dribbled in. Then another and another. To this day, five dollar checks come from out of the blue. No, I haven't made a million, but I've earned back the original investment, several times.

When Chicago's WFLD–TV and I joined forces on a daily television show, they wanted an original idea for promotion. I mentioned the key jewelry, and they liked it. In the past few months, boxes and boxes of Sari's Junkeys have been mailed to columnists, writers, the press and Sari fans. Everyone seems to get a kick out of it. . . .

And that goes to show that you never know when you might use that "junky" idea of yours. Just don't give up hope, and be ready with it when the right opportunity comes along.

✼✼✼✼✼✼✼✼✼✼✼✼✼✼✼✼✼✼✼✼✼✼✼✼

Wooden curtain rings make charming frames for cameos and miniatures.

Maybe you're not out to make a million for yourself, but your club or organization probably needs money-making ideas. There's diamonds in them there junkshops, girls, so follow me. . . .

Wooden curtain rings sell for about a quarter. Anyone can paint them and glue a small round picture to the back. But . . . be a little classy. Buy antique greeting and post-cards. Cut these into miniature pictures and glue them to the rings. Be sure and explain to the prospective buyer at the thrift shop that these miniature pictures are to be hung in groups of not less than four. Suggest that they hang in hallways or foyers and sell them for a dollar apiece.

Everyone loves the ice tongs idea. Just paint a pair and stick a roll of colorful paper toweling between the prongs. (Smaller tongs can hold toilet tissue?) Sell them with a tiny decorative hook for the kitchen or bathroom wall. How much? Oh, about three dollars would net you a profit of a dollar, after expenses (you won't count labor) are subtracted.

Metal shoe lasts come in various sizes because they are

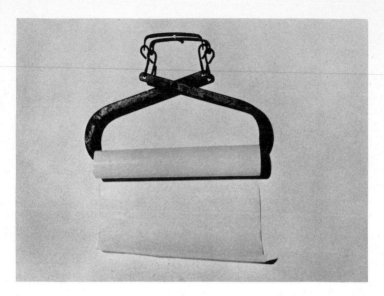

Ice tongs make a perfect paper towel holder.

used to repair all sizes of shoe soles. Floral shops have capitalized on these by painting them and filling the tiny hole on top with a miniature bouquet of flowers. You do the same . . . but with artificial flowers or wooden matches. Sell for two dollars.

Now and then, you'll run across wooden shoe molds. On these, the shoemaker stretched leather for handmade shoes. They're adorable when painted with daises, butterflies, fruits or flowers. Spray them with several coats of shellac and attach them to your front door with eye screws. Sell them as doorknockers, or unique door handles, for three dollars.

Speaking of doorknockers, buy these up in antique and junk shops. Sell them with a guest towel, as a set, for kitchen or bathroom for five dollars. And you'll get it, too.

If your group is really ambitious, and quite talented, have them make tie back collages. Tie backs, you know, are little circles, flowers or figures with a sharp pin on the back. They were made to stick into the wall to hold curtain ties. Today, they sell for about a quarter each. Buy

Wooden shoe molds, before and after the daisy treatment.

flower-styled tiebacks and handpaint them with oils to make them more unusual and colorful.

In any shaped small picture frame, glue material to the cardboard backing. (Velvet or suede cloth makes a lovely backing.) Now, sew plastic leaves to the material. (Stick a large-size needle with button thread right through the cardboard backing on each stitch.) Stick your painted tieback flowers on and put a small cork on the back so the points won't stick your prospective customers. These can sell from five to twenty-five dollars. You're in the big money now!

✹✹✹✹✹✹✹✹✹✹✹✹✹✹✹✹✹✹✹✹✹✹✹✹

Everyone loves a vacation, but I also utilize mine to gather "junk." Stuff from nature that I love to fill my home with. Seaweed (dried), rocks that can be painted or arranged, driftwood, snailshells, pinecones, leaves and plants for drying and preserving. And what could please the kids more than bringing home their "finds," and turning them into . . . things.

A tie back collage. These can take you into the big money.

If you're like me, you'll also drag home cocktail napkins, matchbooks, and other trivia that you can't bear to throw away for fear you'll throw the fun memory out with it. Armed with such paraphernalia after returning from a trip to Carmel, Calif., I knew that if I didn't "collage it," I'd eventually throw it out. The trip meant too much to me to throw out. So, I begged a weathered flat box from the local nurseryman, and sprayed it with antique color enamel. On the back, I glued bits of clippings, postcards, matchbooks, photos, seaweed, leaves, and a ceramic ladybug we had bought at an art fair. The bottom of the box makes a shelf for shells and pinecones. Whenever I pass this collage in our den, it never fails to evoke a smile. How nice if I could build a box for each of our vacations, and just cover a wall with happy memories. Why don't *you* try it?

The children found uses for all the rocks they brought home. Of course, the collectible ones went into Troy's rock collection. The rest became Rock Babies, as we call them. If you've a bored child on your hands, just get some

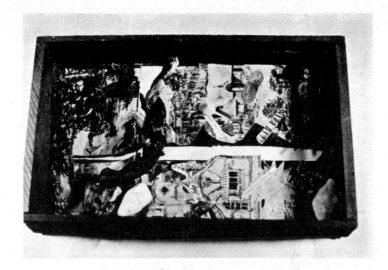

My Carmel, California, collage.

Rock Babies, perfect project for the bored child.

Driftwood doesn't have to be turned into a lamp. It can also be used to make a miniature woodland scene.

irregularly-shaped rocks—rocks that lend themselves to becoming funny people or animals—and spray them with shellac. Now, draw eyes, nose, mouth and hair, using the contours of the rocks as three-dimensional features. Lastly, using poster paint, paint them. Make their clothes polka dotted, or striped. Paint orange hair, purple eyes, Really jazz them up. When they are dry, shoot them again with spray shellac. The kids will love them, and when they're tired of their "Rock Babies," they can always trade them!

We've discovered that most snail shells and pine cones end up either in collages or as Christmas decorations. But what about driftwood? Well, I've never turned it into a lamp . . . yet.

But it's fun to make a miniature woodland scene on driftwood. And the kids can do it, too. I used miniature daisies, cattails, and butterflies from a dimestore giftwrap section; bits of real moss (preserved with hair spray), and a tiny ceramic frog. The fun is in the arranging, carefully gluing and setting-up as natural a scene as you can. You might supply these to a gift shop, once you've filled your home.

✽✽✽✽✽✽✽✽✽✽✽✽✽✽✽✽✽✽✽✽✽✽✽✽

Early to bed, early to rise makes a junkshopper . . . *tired*.

5.

The Flowers that Bloom in the Spring

IT all started when this neighbor of ours heard I was drying flowers with a recipe I'd found in an antique cookbook that was at least a hundred years old. Unfortunately, she requested that I make her a bouquet of home-dried flowers.

Following the instructions on the yellowed page in the old cookbook, I mixed ten cups white cornmeal with two cups borax. Next, I lined the bottom of a deep cardboard box (a husband's laundry shirt boxes work fine) with an inch of this mixture. As the book suggested, I went into the fields "to gather lovely blooms." Not being much of a horticulturist, I wasn't sure what it was I carted home, but I was certain they'd make a lovely bouquet—gold, blue, white and some ivy—but the colors were predominantly gold. Perfect, I thought, for my neighbor's yellow-colored kitchen.

Right here and now, I want to tell you that this is a wonderful old recipe—simple, inexpensive and can be used over and over again for a year. You lay your flowers on the bed of cornmeal in the box, sprinkle the rest of the cornmeal-borax mixture over them until they are completely submerged, and cover the box with a tight-fitting lid.

Next, you leave the box in a cool, dark place for three days. I couldn't figure out where that would be, but I eliminated the refrigerator because I wasn't sure the light went out when the door was closed. At last, in desperation, I slid the box under our king-size bed.

When I removed the dried flowers, I shook them gently to remove all cornmeal. Then I sprayed them with plastic preservative to prevent breakage and deterioration. No matter what technique you use, flowers will fade in drying. But I like the resulting subtle colors, especially when arranged with brightly-painted milkweed pods and bittersweet. But if you prefer a brighter arrangement, try dipping the dried flowers in red or yellow ink.

My neighbor's golden flowers retained their own rich color, and I made them into a beautiful bouquet. I knew I had created a masterpiece and awaited her exuberant response.

"It's nice," she said.

The last I saw of her that sunny afternoon, she was seated in her living room, gingerly holding my bouquet on her lap.

Later in the week I received a rather cool telephone call from her. She said she'd had to throw the bouquet out. It made her sneeze. To this day, she's not speaking to me. She's certain that I gave her ragweed on purpose. What do you think?

But my poor husband. He had to explain to the dermatologist that he'd contacted poison ivy from the weeds "under our bed." And would you believe it, the doctor wanted to know why he'd married a "grass widow"!

From that same antique cookbook, I learned that in days gone by they preserved bittersweet, cranberry bushes and the like with equal parts glycerin (which can be obtained from your pharmacy) and water. The stems, when soaked in this solution for three days, will not deteriorate for six months to two years.

But I wanted a tree. Long before the decorating magazines started "showing" trees in livingrooms, dens, foyers and patios, I knew that a home is not a home without a tree. And, quite by accident, I discovered how to make an artificial tree, thus saving myself $60 to $500, depending on the size tree I otherwise would have purchased. And, you as I, would certainly otherwise have purchased one. Right?

Armed with a hatchet, go into the woods and select a tree with many artistic branches. (Ours is ceiling to

A home is not a home without a tree. Here's mine, with artificial leaves sewn on.

floor and six feet wide.) Cut it down. When you've been released from jail, or as soon as possible, set the stump end of your tree in a quart can of antifreeze. In three days, remove the tree and set it in a large container, supported by rocks, gravel, soil or what have you. I had the children gather small rocks and we boiled them in water and bleach. (Serve that to your bridge club some afternoon. . . .)

Eventually, the leaves will fall off. But the tree will not dry out and become a fire hazard. Nor will it attract any unwelcome visitors such as termites. If you wish, you may decorate your tree as I did: Purchase artificial leaves at a discount or dime store; trim the leaves from the plastic branches, and sew them, one by one, to your tree with heavy-duty button thread. It *only* takes about six hours.

When my husband put a stockade fence up behind our house, I wanted it to be covered with ivy. Immediately! So that night I crept into the woods and cut down young grapevines. These I dragged home and soaked in glycerin and water. I then looped them all over the fence, and round and round the posts. In three days the vines dried as hard as iron bars. One moonless night I sewed artificial grape leaves on. (You might try this the next time you have insomnia. . . .)

You can imagine how astounded the neighbors were about my "instant vines." But you should see the cars that go round and round our block when there's three feet of snow on the gound. (Have *you* ever seen grapevines blooming in mid-winter?)

✠✠✠✠✠✠✠✠✠✠✠✠✠✠✠✠✠✠✠✠✠✠✠

Junking each day keeps those doldrums away!

6.

You'll Never Be a Millionaire Without a Magnet

Now, the fun starts! You've dried and preserved your flowers and trees and you need imaginative containers to arrange them in. Head to the junkshops, trading posts, antique shops, auctions, garage and rummage sales, or anyplace where there could be a bargain (and the off-chance of picking-up a real treasure by accident.)

Are you the type who will take a gamble? Prove it. See if you can correctly identify the container in the picture on the next page. That's right. It's part of a poker-dice game. The part that shakes the dice.

When I found this item on the fifty-cent bargain table at the Wagon Wheel Trading Post in Lisle, Ill., I thought it was brass. To make certain, I pulled a little magnet from my purse and held it against the metal. If the magnet will *not* stick, it's real brass, copper, sterling silver or gold. And who wants anything else. Right?

Your next question might logically be, "How do you clean filthy brass?" My favorite way for cleaning tarnished brass is to wash it in pure ammonia and then polish with a clean, dry cloth.

A poker-dice shaker . . .

When brass has turned green or has been painted, I soak it in a strong paint and varnish stripper or remover. I've never seen a label that suggested you could do this, but it works quite well if you pour the whole can of stripper into an old potato chip can; add a little water, if necessary; and submerge your brass or copper item in this overnight. (If your "find" is too large for a container, brush stripper on frequently and let set.) In the morning, rinse your treasure under cool water. Shine it with a clean dry rag. You'll be thrilled with the results. There will be little or no scrubbing for you to do. All paint and grime will have floated off. This method will remove up to three coats of paint from brass or copper. (Never use stripper on silver or gold.)

Stripper *is* expensive, so save the liquid in the potato chip can for the next time you strip—furniture, of course.

Because of this brass-cleaning secret, I garnered a bargain in Chicago's Old Town last spring. I remember finding a pair of candle sconces despite the gloom in a wonderful old junk barn on Wells Street. Even now, I can almost smell the odors that clung to everything there.

. . . becomes a charming centerpiece holder.

A heady mixture of sawdust, dry leaves and succulent apples, it stimulated my treasure-hunting instincts. I began to tingle like a geiger counter near uranium.

Nonchalantly, I waited for my moment. The dealer turned his head to another customer. In a flash, I'd held my little magnet against the back of one of the old light fixtures that could, with a little work, become candle sconces. It was strongly repelled; beneath all that old paint was solid, antique brass.

Daintily, I lifted one filthy fixture by its spidery wiring, carried it in my well-manicured hand and laid it disdainfully at the dealer's feet.

"How much is this icky old thing?"

"Three dollars."

"But it's so dirty. . . ."

"Three dollars."

"And all that old wiring. . . ."

"Three dollars."

"But it's covered in layers and layers of old paint!"

"Three dollars."

"I'll give you five dollars for the pair."

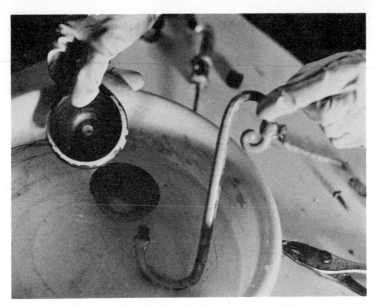

A dip in stripper . . .

. . . and old parts (left) become like new (right).

The old sconce and the new.

"Five fifty."

"Sold."

You see, you can still get a bargain if you're smart enough. . . .

That evening, having removed the wiring with plyers and screw driver, I plopped my "finds" into the potato chip can of stripper. If that paint didn't peel off, I'd lost money. If it did, the sconces could be worth up to $200. At least that's what many interior decorators charge for these popular accessories.

Morning found my sconces completely clean of paint and dirt. I inserted twenty-five-cent candle converters into each of the four lightbulb sockets, hung the sconces on our foyer wall, and added candles. They were lovely! And as I told hubby: "It's like owning a good blue chip stock. Solid antique brass can't help but go up in value!"

❋❋❋❋❋❋❋❋❋❋❋❋❋❋❋❋❋❋❋❋❋❋❋❋

And remember . . . the name of the game is "new it yourself."

7.

Let Me Help You Light the Way

DID you know that the "in crowd" is buying up old sewing machines? They tear-off the wood (saving it for collages) and use the ornate iron legs for tables . . . and tables . . . and tables. For instance, when topped with a ½- or one-inch-thick slab of marble, sewing machine legs make an elegant buffet table for your dining room. In a foyer, flanked by an antique mirror, a smaller version of the same table provides a marvelous island for freshening make-up and hair, or for tossing gloves and scarves on. A very feminine bedroom would look enchanting with a marble desk with sewing-machine legs. White-painted legs add a touch of French New Orleans to a patio.

In case you can't find a piece of scrap marble to suit your needs or your budget, have a ¼-inch piece of glass cut to size. Glue on contact paper that comes in a marble pattern. Smooth it down, and if any bubbles appear, punch tiny pin holes in them. Spray with several coats of shellac. Would you believe that only an expert can tell the difference?

Marci Braun and I re-assembling an old sewing machine stand on TV.

Or, you might stain the glass with any of the liquid plastic products available at hobby shops. One inexpensive stain is used for painting the backs of glass aquariums. Ask for it at your local pet shop. You brush it on the glass, and it dries forming crystals like frost. To make a stained-glass window effect, outline your design with black oil paint. When dry, fill in the design with any colors of liquid plastic you choose. (It comes in about ten colors.)

Incidentally, you can stain your glass shower door, windows, bottles and glass tables, and remove the stain with vinegar and water when you're tired of it.

I'll never forget the day I found a box of clear glass bottles in a local antique shop. They were about five inches high, squarish, stoppered and very antique looking.

The dealer said they were French perfume bottles, and I could have the whole box for five dollars. Do you know, dollar signs actually danced before my eyes. I could just see those bottles stained and decorated with

43

My "French" perfume bottles—five dollars for the box.

liquid plastic, and selling for double my initial investment. Aha! At last I was on my way to that first million.

Later, while brushing on the liquid plastic, I saw tiny little print on the bottom of a bottle. It said MADE IN JAPAN.

For heavens sake, save your glass bug bombs at the end of the summer. One fall, I striped these in multiple colors of stain and filled them with tiny, decorative perfumed soaps. Add a bow and perhaps a nosegay of flowers and you have a charming, inexpensive gift for a hostess, club exchange or someone who needs a bath.

✱✱✱✱✱✱✱✱✱✱✱✱✱✱✱✱✱✱✱✱✱✱✱✱

As you may know, I'm a TV celebrity. (Everytime I say that, I laugh, cross my fingers and, for that matter, my eyes, too.) One of my most thrilling experiences was attending my first TV Awards dinner. . . .

I remember a mirage of beautiful people . . . people in granny glasses and fur boas, minks and silk hostess pajamas, glittery low-cut minis; Bermuda tuxedos. . . .

As a novice in this business, I could easily have felt lost in such a crowd. But I didn't, for I'd risen to the occasion. Not with my gown, but with a special "junk-shopper" touch—beautiful four-inch-long crystal earrings. Between you and me, I borrowed two glass prisms from an old chandelier. I glued these to screw-type earring backs from the hobby shop (12 cents). When I'd stained them to match my gown, they refracted every light in shades of turquoise.

Now and then, most of us have a chance to be elegant. Girls, don't ever back down. With your imagination, find a way to steal a teeny-weeny bit of the show and sneak into the spotlight. Why not? Like ideas, life is free for the taking.

⚜⚜⚜⚜⚜⚜⚜⚜⚜⚜⚜⚜⚜⚜⚜⚜⚜⚜⚜⚜⚜⚜

Preparing for my first TV Awards dinner.

My groovy stained-glass lamp, together with a high-button-shoe flower holder.

Once again, liquid stain came to the rescue when Don and I found a metal lamp. It grew from a heap of junk on the floor in a trading post. It looked like any dirty old lamp but for its square metal shade that had probably held stained-glass in days past.

Don paid two dollars for it. I cleaned it, and as I swabbed the black metal with ammonia, it turned to copper right before my eyes. To say we were delighted with a solid copper lamp is an understatement. We replaced the material in the shade with regular window glass, and stained it with liquid plastic. The lamp is groovy. But friends of ours adored it, and when they got transferred to New York we let them have it. I hope they still treasure our treasure as much as we did.

Lamp people say that kerosene lamps are popular once again. Antique collectors restore them and fill them with one of the colored, scented oils. But I committed the impardonable sin: I had one electrified for our bedroom.

Campers use kerosene lanterns. But my wonderful mother (who doesn't particularly like to camp) turns lanterns into "camp" light fixtures for your home. So I bid on a kerosene lantern at a farm auction. This thing should have been condemned, but I ended up gingerly laying it in the trunk of my car. Believe me, no one

My mom, Mrs. Alice Milner, and I working on a kerosene lantern. The finished product is on the right.

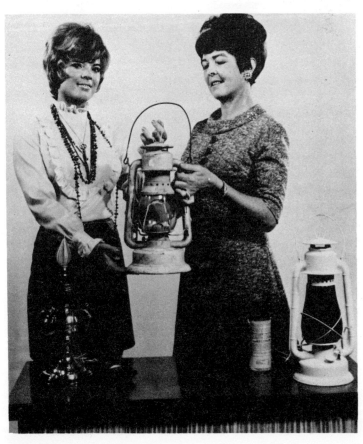

thought it could become anything, but Mom.

She showed me how to scrub it with steel wool and cleanser. I showed her how to remove excess rust with equal parts vinegar and water. It still looked lousy. After three coats of very thick enamel, it began to shape up. I stained the chimney with liquid plastic and Don electrified it. Now it hangs on an arm in my son's bedroom. And to think, it only cost a total of five dollars . . . three fingernails, two sleepless nights, and a cup of perspiration. What a bargain?

Another time I bought a very peculiar-looking lamp

My romantic candleholder, after I had removed the priceless original wiring and bulb.

about a foot high, but it was clean. It was made of hammered metal and had a bell-like chimney hanging over a very ugly cylindrical lightbulb. I threw the bulb and wiring in the garbage and placed a candle in the empty socket. Now it was a romantic addition to our dining room table.

Shortly after that, a neighbor (who happens to know all about antique lamps) dropped by.

"That happens to be a real antique," she intoned, pointing to my romantic candleholder. "It's one of the first light fixtures ever made. Too bad it didn't have the original cylindrical bulb and wiring. It'd be worth a fortune to a museum or a collector."

And here's another cute lamp story. . . . It's the rage to buy old metal floorlamps for a dollar or so, just for the ornate metal base. Remove the base (usually it screws off) and give it a good scrubbing with a wire brush. Spray with a base coat of rust preventative paint and a final coat of any color you wish. Now, say you've found two of these ornate bases, and one's just a bit smaller than the other. Tip the smaller one upside down and screw it to the larger one that's right side up. You now have a beautiful compote fruit bowl.

There's one gal in the Chicago area who started constructing these and selling them for eight to twelve dollars apiece. She supplies boutiques and department stores. They're absolutely beautiful . . . especially when they're free for the making yourself.

✳✳✳✳✳✳✳✳✳✳✳✳✳✳✳✳✳✳✳✳✳✳✳✳

It's fairly common for one to run across an original sculpture in junk and antique shops. Often, they're cracked, chipped or discolored. But maybe, like me, someday you'll splurge and buy a new statue. Gingerly, you'll carry it home and watch it "self-destruct" as a child knocks it to the floor. You can do lots of things at a time like that—throw something at the child, throw the child at something, or throw yourself out the window.

49

Somehow, I managed not to do any of these. Instead, I clamped my jaw determinedly, took-up tweezers and glued the sculpture back together. During that hour of tedious labor, the doors were locked, the phone was off the hook and I did not breathe. The end result was a statue with only a few chips missing, and many little cracks running all over it.

Certainly, I knew, paint would not hide those hideous cracks. But, I wondered, what about paint sprinkled with sand? No, something handier. Why not table salt? And it worked! Wet paint, sprinkled with table salt, then when dry, lightly spray-painted again, gives a statue, vase, ashtray, or anything, a hand-carved sandstone effect!

George was one of my statues who, when renovated via table salt, became a popular relic. Not only did the TV studio where my daily show originates ask if they could use George as a permanent part of the set, but he was adopted by the children in our neighborhood.

It all started because some cad put me in charge of the Monster Booth at our gradeschool Fun Fair. Now anything to do with PTA was a novelty to me because my children were just getting into school. I wasn't quite sure how to start, but I knew that I wanted my Monster Booth to be the creepiest in the history of Fun Fairs. (Incidentally, the purpose of the Monster Booth is to make money by making-up children to look like pirates, gouls and hippies.)

About this time, I chanced to find a huge decaying bust of a rather unattractive man. Four dollars, some table salt and antique-color paint and he was . . . different. When I set him on a high pedestal table, he glowered down at all comers to my booth. Then I added Ben Franklin specs, glued on a few yellow buckteeth, sprinkled catsup on an old beard and tied it on, and plopped a ratty indian braid wig on his head.

On the wall behind George, I arranged fish net spiderwebs (sprayed black) crawling with huge black cardboard spiders. Along the floor, psychedelic octupi, snakes

"Good old George," after the table-salt, antique-paint treatment.

and crabs writhed menacingly. When I was finished, the booth was so hideous that smaller children wouldn't enter. How embarrassed I was when parents encouraged their children to enter for a make-up session, and they'd hide and cry. I'd outsmarted myself. But the older kids loved it, and they still ask about "good old George."

They haven't asked me to do a booth at the Fun Fair again. Is there a method to my madness? I'll never tell.

✲✲✲✲✲✲✲✲✲✲✲✲✲✲✲✲✲✲✲✲✲✲✲✲

From now on, the junk you save may be your own!

8.

How to Get Beautiful,
Curvaceous Legs

Y OU'VE probably seen old tablelegs in your local antique shop selling for about five dollars each. Knowing this, you'll agree (I'm certain) that I was very fortunate to find a heap of junk and furniture in the street near our home. I asked if this was a flea market sale like they have in Paris, but a neighbor explained that it was Spring Clean-up, an annual event when everyone spruced up his garage, attic and basement, leaving the discards in a heap for the junkman.

Well, I'm not a junkwoman, but . . . can you blame me if I just put a few things in the trunk of my car. And you know, by the time I got home I had thirty table legs!

(Did you know that, nowadays, in many shops, they actually take the legs off the tables and sell them separately because they can get more money that way?)

I've seen many things done with table legs, but two of the most attractive ideas are turning them into table-lamps, via wiring and adding a shade, and into giant floor-type candleholders by nailing a wooden salad bowl to the top and painting it to match the leg. Add a fat, colorful candle and a cluster of artificial grapes, and you have a decorator's accessory.

But my favorite idea was when I screwed two of these heavy, ornate table legs together, end to end, making a five-foot-high column. I made fifteen of these columns, attaching each to our patio fence at twelve-foot intervals. Now, with grapevines and columns decorating our patio, it started to look like an Italian garden, which was just what I wanted.

The legs needed a finish that could withstand rain, sun and snow. It was about this time that a national paint company chose me to be the "Paint Lady of the Year." (Isn't that glamorous?) My prize was all the free paint I want for life, and a paint roller. Just what I've always wanted.

They designed a brochure about Junkshooping with Sari; perhaps you've seen it in your local hardware or paint store. Most important, the brochure tells about the new antique paint colors that all the paint companies are coming out with.

The most popular color comes in a spray can and it's designed for people who don't want to strip furniture. It's called Antique. And the color is neither black nor brown, but a mixture of the two. I call it . . . mud. Mud blends with most woods, and it was perfect for my columns.

Shortly after that, I was meandering through another shop and I saw—you guessed it—more table legs. These were small, ornately carved end table and coffee table legs. I really got a bargain this time—fifteen legs for $2.80. I turned them over and attached them to my columns. Now that they were painted and attractive, I had . . . absolutely nothing. But I was getting somewhere. And that's how it goes when you're creating with junk, or anything . . . things just fall together, piece by piece.

In another antique shop, I found some small, round jello molds. I sprayed them flat black and nailed one on each of the table legs attached to the columns. Now, in

Touching up my table-leg, jello-mold, bug-repellant lanterns.

my imagination, I could visualize pots of ivy and geraniums setting in each mold. Wouldn't they make beautiful planters!

It occurred to me that these planters could be blown off in a heavy wind. Undoubtedly, they'd land on one of my children's heads. So I waited, keeping my eyes open for something lightweight, weatherproof and decorative. While browsing through a unique floral-gift shop in the city, I found just what I needed—plastic swimming pool bug bombs!

Have you ever seen them? They're colorful—red, blue,

green, yellow and white—little lanterns with a bug repellent candle and a weight inside. Naturally, they're meant to float in a swimming pool.

Now, evenings when we eat out on our patio, I take a long match and light each of the little lanterns sitting in the jello molds on my table leg "candalabra arms." Not only do we have a soft, romantic glow all through the evening, but we don't have a single bug within two blocks of our home. How *can* you with twelve bug bombs going?

Oh yes, my husband has another suggestion for table legs. He says they make wonderful logs for the fire. . . .

✤✤✤✤✤✤✤✤✤✤✤✤✤✤✤✤✤✤✤✤✤✤✤✤

There's more to every piece of junk than meets the eye. Take another look at it!

9.

Let's Have a Cook-In

THERE'S no end to the creative ideas from the junkshop for your patio. For instance, how about this: Find an old water heater holder and a tractor seat and turn them into a chair. Water heater holders are cast iron, hour-glass-shaped frames that are usually two or three feet high. About seven dollars, they're easy to find, but usually pretty rusty. First, brush off all excess rust and debris with a wire bristle brush. Then scrub the holder with equal parts vinegar and water. When dry, spray on a base coat of rust preventative paint. When this is dry, paint your water heater holder orange or red or any bright color that will "mod-up" your patio or den.

At an auction or a country junkyard, seek out an old tractor seat. These are *always* rusty and sell for between three and five dollars. Give the seat the same treatment that you gave the water heater holder. Solder the seat to the top of the holder and—*voila!*—you have a "camp" chair for a wall-hung, fold-out desk, a unique chair for a den or patio table, or a stool for a breakfast counter. Even one "tractor seat chair" adds the right touch to a small apartment.

Incidentally, as often happens with a really good idea, spontaneous discovery occurred. Individuals from different parts of the country created it on their own, as evidenced by the variety of magazines and newspapers it suddenly appeared in.

Water heater holders make darling patio tables, too. Top them with a mosaic tray. Just find an old round tray of wood, plastic or metal. (Mine cost a quarter in a junk-shop.) Glue on small squares of mosaic tile in any pattern you wish. Grout between the tiles and let dry. Now seal with several coats of weatherproof spray shellac. Borrow some of dad's coin collection or brother's butterfly collection and glue these to the tray, too. Seal the whole thing, again, with weatherproof shellac. It's striking!

Mosaic tray, before and after.

You're like me if summer turns you on. You like wood-sies and the cookouts that go with them. But dragging a stupid bag of charcoal around or nestling a can of extremely flammable, combustible liquid starter is definitely not your thing.

So . . . do something about it. Find an old coal shuttle, give it the rust clean-up treatment, a coat of rust preventative paint and two final coats of antique black. Fill the shuttle three-quarters with briquettes, set the starter on top, and toss-in several books of matches. Now you're ready to burn, baby.

But what about those "coal miner hands" after a session of manually transferring briquettes to the grill? (Sure, you tried to pour the whole bag into the pot, but the majority hit the grass and only three went on the grill.) Obviously you need a shovel. And did you know there is such an animal? I mean, if you're lucky, you'll find a rusty old coal shuttle shovel in an antique shop for three dollars. Or, you might buy a brand new camp shovel in one of those wonderful backwoods-fishing-camp general stores for just a dollar. Either way, give it a dose of vinegar and a dash of paint. Now you're really swinging. With a small shovel for your coal shuttle, you're bound to succeed at being a sophisticated shuttle bug!

(And have you even seen a coal shuttle filled with chipped ice and used as a champagne or wine cooler? It's groovy. Try it sometime.)

One of our annual summer rituals has always been the slow but certain destruction of a newly purchased, metal barbecue grill. We don't have to look at the calendar to know that it's late August. One glance at the rusty, charred flooring in our grill and we know that summer is on its way out. You see, unlike most people, we rarely remember to line the bottom of our grills with gravel or fire base. And since we took up camping, that's just one more thing for someone to remember to throw into the car. And someone never does. . . .

Well, Don has cured all that now. Recently, on one of

My mom and I demonstrating how to transform an old coal scuttle.

the rare occasions when he accompanies me junkshopping, he saw a huge old iron pot. He smiled a little uncertainly, as he walked around it, sizing it up. He frowned, kicked it, then bought it for twelve dollars.

Let me mention right here that this whole project was kept top secret. Not a word escaped the artist's lips as he dragged that old pot to our car. (Now, let's admit it, girls, when we have an idea we tell the world. We try it out on anyone who'll listen. We nod agreeably at their suggestions, then we do exactly what we want. Right?) The twinkle in Don's eyes told me he had a great idea, and I was wise enough to keep my mouth shut.

No fancy chemicals for Don. He cleaned that old pot with a wire brush, the water from a garden hose, and plenty of elbow grease. (But then, he's got the muscle to do that sort of thing.) He lined the bottom with gravel, heaped the pot full of driftwood, and placed, a round wire barbecue grill across the top. (Although I objected to this mundane use of my beautiful driftwood, I still kept my mouth shut.)

When ignited, this firepot permeated our little suburban community with a most heavenly aroma. Pure sandalwood, I thought, and it reminded me of my Bali Hai—Carmel, California.

✶✶✶✶✶✶✶✶✶✶✶✶✶✶✶✶✶✶✶✶✶✶✶

Would you believe that anyone would want a grotesque red-and-green-painted, peeling, cement, 300-pound antique water fountain? Well I did, so I bid on it at an auction and got it for twenty dollars.

Two men delivered it in two parts to our patio. I was certain the neighbors were aghast worrying about property depreciation . . . and I couldn't blame them. It had looked like such a buy at the auction, but now, sitting in our lovely Italian garden, it looked just plain awful. I had two hours before Don was due in from work. . . .

With a wire brush, I loosened all the peeling paint. Armed with the widest paint brush obtainable, I started slopping whitewash all over that massive cement monster. All of a sudden, it looked lovely. The white paint brought out the graceful lines of the statue that sits in the middle of the four-foot-wide fountain, and I noticed graceful sculpting all over the pedestal bottom and around the sides of the bowl-shaped fountain top.

Would you believe that Don liked it? In fact, he rigged a hose and copper tubing through the thing. Then he asked me to turn it on. *Voila!* Water squirted twenty-feet high.

"That's how we water the backyard," he explained.

Second gear on the fountain is a gentle, trickle that sounds romantic on a hot, summer night. Of course we added goldfish and lilly pads. And the fountain has paid for itself. Guests just can't resist throwing in a wishing penny, and naturally, I gather them up quite regularly and put them in a piggy bank.

A "wagon wheel planter" is an especially good idea for your patio, lawn or garden. To make this unique planter, get a large sewer pipe from a construction materials supply house. Place a wagonwheel across this and paint

Our 300-pound antique water fountain, after rehabilitation.

the two bright red. From the florist, get appropriately-sized clay flowerpots and nestle them between the rungs all the way around the wheel. Plant these with anything you wish. However, strawberries thrive in this environment because the drainage is good, there's plenty of sun and they can climb all over the wheel. Your imagination can tell you more about the beauty of this planter than any picture I might paint.

I nestled small flowerpots between the wheel's rungs and planted them with basil, chives, mint, rosemary, thyme and parsley. Believe me, you can't help but impress your dinner guests when you sweep across the kitchen in your long hostess gown, daintily snip fresh basil from your wagon wheel planter, and toss it into the spaghetti sauce. It also makes a darling winter garden.

✹✹✹✹✹✹✹✹✹✹✹✹✹✹✹✹✹✹✹✹✹✹✹

Would you believe it if you were driving along and you saw this beautiful hand-carved old cabinet setting out by the garbage? Wouldn't you knock on the door and ask if you could have that "horrible old thing" as long as they're throwing it out anyway? Certainly you would. If you were a junkshopper.

And, lucky me, it turned out to be a very rare telephone cabinet. The woman was kind enough to give me the tiny chair that goes with it, too. Both of these, I stripped on the patio. A week later, a foot of grass died around the edge of our cement patio. Don didn't like it. And, furthermore, don't use stripper on an asphalt driveway. It bubbles to mush. Best to strip on a cement garage floor with a water drain nearby.

Anyway, I replanted the grass, and refinished the cabinet and chair with paste shoe polish. Because these cabinets have slots inside for telephone books and a tiny French phone, and a drawer for pencils and stuff, I turned mine into a file cabinet for my various (ahem) businesses. I've been told that the original French phone was brass and is very hard to find. Imagine how delighted I was

The rare telephone cabinet I rescued from the garbage.

when Don gave me a music box copy of just such a phone.

You know, I seriously believe that all antique collectors desire to own at least one old clock. Women like them because of the beauty and sentimentality of antique clocks. Men like them because they are handmade, precision instruments.

I bought a 108-year-old clock that loudly (very, very loudly) chimed the hours. It looked charming on top of my telephone cabinet . . . until it stopped working.

Don was happy about this, because at last he could get some sleep. I was disappointed. But the antique dealer explained that if such a clock is just a little bit off balance, it'll go tick-tick, tock-tock, or tock-tick. Then it'll stop running. So you have to slide a matchbook under it, until it is balanced, and it goes tick-tock, tick-tock. I wasn't quite sure who was off balance—the clock, me, or the antique dealer. Either way, Don stole the chime mechanism and now my clock just sits there looking old and pretty.

✳✳✳✳✳✳✳✳✳✳✳✳✳✳✳✳✳✳✳✳✳✳✳✳

Very few people are lucky enough to find a ten-foot-long chicken coop for a dollar. And get to strap it to the roof of their car and actually carry it home. But I was one of these, possibly the only one.

The coop, covered with chicken feathers and—well, you know what—was of very wormy pine wood. Just the kind of wood the furniture manufacturers work so hard to copy with their "distressed" furniture finish. I hosed it down, let it dry and painted it a dark, rich brown. I antiqued it with black paste shoe polish spread on with cheese cloth.

Across the back wall of our dining room there's this beautiful bookcase that everyone "ooh's" and "aah's" over. Guess what it is. . . .

I love shutters, so you can imagine how excited I got about a pair of unique outdoor-type shutters selling for four dollars. I gave these the same brown, antique black finish as the chicken coop, and hinged them to the inside of the dining room window. I like to see out. I mean, heavy drapes are lovely, so long as you can open them and let the outdoors come in.

Stained glass would have been a lovely backing for the shutters, but it was too heavy. Then, in a gift shop in Bloomington, Ill., I saw a roll of white oriental rice paper. I knew that if the paper was embedded with real bamboo leaves, it would be enchanting as a background for the frame shutters. I cut the rice paper carefully and thumb-

Believe it or not—a chicken coop. Price: $1.00.

tacked it on. Today, the sun can stream in, but we have privacy, too.

✸✸✸✸✸✸✸✸✸✸✸✸✸✸✸✸✸✸✸✸✸✸✸

I'm proud when people admire my fireplace hearth. I'm even proud of it when I'm sitting home alone writing, and I can't help but smile at "it." "It" being a roly-poly orange fireplace I've installed in the middle of our living room floor. I've always wanted one, and, finally, I convinced the "boss" to let me have it.

First, though, knowing how logical he is, I did some research about the safety precautions for the construction of a fireplace and hearth. I hoped this would impress him. It did. He told me to go ahead and install the darn thing, but if the house burned down it was my fault.

A little less enthusiastically, I wandered through the local junkshops looking for something to strike me, hard, in the way of "hearth-building" material. At last, I sighted a huge old oak table top about five feet by six feet. "One dollar," the dealer said, and he even loaded it into my car.

Don and I adding a log to our fireplace hearth. Behind it is my oriental garden, and on the wall are my stained glass windows.

But, you say, wood burns. You're right. So, I set the table top in the livingroom, just where the fireplace would be installed two days hence. Then I returned to scouring the antique shops and (you won't believe this but it's true) I found a box of red, clay fireplace tiles for a dollar. I felt it was an omen that the house might not burn down.

I glued the tiles to the table top, and grouted between them. The masonry work was pretty good, if I may say so myself. (But now I'm taking a teaspoon of prepared mustard daily because that's supposed to help restore damaged fingernails.)

Now, the artist in me really went to work. Was the three-foot space behind the fireplace going to waste? I asked myself. Waste not, want not. So I hauled in two bags of red pebbles, red patio stones, and some volcanic rock. (Remember, girls, do become friends with the boys in the neighborhood. Loan them your motorcycle, and they'll help you haul heavy things in.)

My stained glass windows before they were completely stripped.

Now, I had the beginnings of an oriental garden in shades of red to match the hearth. I arranged our shell, driftwood and rock and fossil collections in realistic "natural" confusion. I added ferns, ivy and a six-foot preserved tree. There are also frogs, toads, a butterfly and birds. Believe me, the naturalists at Field Museum have never created a more authentic-looking desert-mountain-woodland scene in a six-by-three-foot area. It's really . . . something.

A terrarium in a blue wine jug added a nice touch to the hearth, so did a brass "fireplace tool" set from London. But the best accent was made from ancient railroad windows. These beautiful stained glass windows had been in a fire. In fact, after stripping them for two days, I was certain they were in several fires. But, down deep, very, very deep, beneath all that . . . gunk, there was wood. Beautiful, beautiful walnut. So I planed the wood, sanded it, and refinished it with paste shoe polish. I hinged these to the wall behind the fireplace to look like a real window. What do you see when you look out that window? Carmel, California, of course, what would you expect?

❀❀❀❀❀❀❀❀❀❀❀❀❀❀❀❀❀❀❀❀❀❀❀❀❀

Happiness is unloading your car full of junk before your husband gets home.

10.

Gifts Can Be Groovy

MY poor in-laws—it's rare when I pur-
chase a Christmas gift for anyone. Actually, I feel it's an
insult. So, I start designing gifts about September (sort of
a subconscious thing). Garage and yard sales are prevalent
at the time, and I stock up on miscellaneous pieces of
whatnots and junk that might come in handy later.

Recently, I found two tiny antique pill boxes for a quarter each. When the magnet wouldn't stick to them, I knew
they were brass or sterling silver. After boiling potatoes
one night, I set the boxes in the potato water. They
cleaned up immediately. I had the silver lids engraved
with each of our grandmothers' initials. They'll love these
when I frame their grandchildren's pictures in them.

�֍֍֍֍֍֍֍֍֍֍֍֍֍֍֍֍֍֍֍֍֍֍֍

One very original idea developed from a cigar mold.
When I purchased this, I thought it was just a curiosity.
When I had cleaned it with Flax soap and a soft cloth,
the pine wood glistened softly, reminding me of pioneers.
Aha! I know a woman who collects primitive antiques and
early American accessories. She'd love this . . . if I could
think of a practical use for it. I recalled that she had a

A cigar mold becomes a perfect holder for antique utensils.

collection of miniature spoons, and this clue was all I needed. You might try this—glue the two sections of the cigar mold together, attach a brass eagle decoration to the front, and a wall hanger to the back. Now, slide several ornate spoons into the cigar molds on top. You can bet that anyone would love this unique gift.

Do you think my friend liked it? No, because I never gave it to her. I kept it for myself.

❋❋❋❋❋❋❋❋❋❋❋❋❋❋❋❋❋❋❋❋❋❋❋

Have you got a handsome bachelor friend on your shopping list? Has he got everything? Why don't you find an old U.S. Post Office Box door. You remember all the darling pigeonholes? With brass doors and combination locks? Now these are sold in antique shops, and usually are not too expensive.

Clean the brass with a little household ammonia and fine steel wool. Remove the old decal letters from the tiny glass window in the brass frame.

Give this to "handsome," suggesting that he install it in his front door so he can take a peek before he opens it. After all, he'll want to check just which date is calling. It

An old U.S. Post Office Box door can even be used as a mail box, of all things.

The fruits of rubbling—hand-carved moldings.

makes a good mail box, too. The postman just drops the mail thru. Or, best of all (if you're single, that is), mount your picture in the frame and give it to him.

※※※※※※※※※※※※※※※※※※※※※※※※

Another way to pick up unique junk for gifts is to go rubbling. Get together with several friends and wander through old buildings and mansions that are being torn down. You'll find hand-carved moldings, ornate plaster moldings and columns, newel posts, bannisters, barnsiding, wooden shingles and just about anything you need.

Moldings also make charming shelf supports.

One dreary March day when I was teaching a course called "Junk Artistry" at a YMCA in Chicago, I read about a fire in an antique shop on Wells Street.

"Class," I said, "we're going on a field trip today. We're going to learn the art of rubbling."

And we hit it rich! Sodden, having been nearly electrocuted more than once, smudged with soot, we emerged from the burnt-out building with armloads of treasures that cost us nothing. The sculpted plaster moldings I picked up usually sell for fifteen dollars apiece. Of course I had to scrub the soot off, but they would become bookends or a very quaint shelf for someone for Christmas.

✣✣✣✣✣✣✣✣✣✣✣✣✣✣✣✣✣✣✣✣✣✣✣

Certain gift ideas are easy to find in the shops near your home. One of these is a washboard. But I went all the way to Galena, Ill., to find my washboard. And it was worth it. This historical old resort town is interesting for anyone, but for a junkshopper . . . wow!

I promised my husband I'd boat with him on the Mississippi River by Galena one day if he'd accompany me through the antique shops and museums on another. It was a deal. Galena, or bust!

Sunburned and happy, we docked our little boat and drove to the hotel. An authentic mansion, the Belvedere Hotel is completely restored, down to the very silver on the tables. We slept in a huge bed that you climbed into via handcarved mahogany steps. Our clothes hung in wardrobes, rather than closets. It was groovy.

By mid-morning the next day, I realized that most of Galena is being restored to its past splendor by private families. Many of these, it turns out, are young couples from Chicago who like to junkshop. The shops weren't as cheap as I'd hoped, but I did purchase a brass scrub board and a 100-year-old tin lunchbox called a grauer.

There's nothing like that moment when you pour ammonia over dirty metal and it turns, instantly, into shining brass. That's just what happened to my washboard. I painted the wooden frame gold, too.

If it had been an ordinary scrub board, I'd have turned it into a bulletin board. You've seen that done, I'm sure. You screw hooks into the wooden frame for keys and things. Miniature magnets stick to the metal center part and hold notes to it. It makes a cute gift.

Magnets won't stick to brass, so I couldn't turn my washboard into a bulletin board. When I'd thought about it awhile, I decided that we all have some hand laundry, so I'd keep my scrub board for just that. But it would also be a feminine accessory for a charming bathroom.

Greeting cards and wrapping paper gave me ideas for a flower motif for the wooden frame on my scrub board. I held a real violet over white paper and traced the shadow. I cut this out and traced it with lead pencil until the frame was solid with flower designs. Using iridescent pink nail enamel and red, white and green oil paints, I created leaves, stems and flowers.

I added a red velvet rose, and the washboard was ready for a gift for my sister-in-law. This would also make a darling shower gift, accompanying a good silk slip, for instance.

✶✶✶✶✶✶✶✶✶✶✶✶✶✶✶✶✶✶✶✶✶✶✶

It seems everyone's tin painting lately. Milk cans, pitchers, berry pails and lunchboxes make wonderful gifts when oil painted with flowers, fruits and butterflies. My first experience at tin painting was on the old grauer I'd picked-up at Galena. Since then, I've adorned clothes boilers and bread boxes with my designs. The former make nice magazine racks; the latter, good toaster covers.

But the old lunch pail became a purse. To begin with,

Some painted tin, including my lunch pail purse.

it was unique. The bottom section had been made to hold beer; the top, sandwiches. I gave it several coats of antique-color paint. Next, I drew butterflies and grapes and painted them every color of the rainbow and sealed the whole thing with several coats of shellac.

People actually stop me on the street—and ask where I got that darling purse. Best of all, I saw one selling for twenty-five dollars at a fancy shop on Michigan Avenue. And it wasn't nearly as cute as mine (in my opinion).

✳✳✳✳✳✳✳✳✳✳✳✳✳✳✳✳✳✳✳✳✳✳✳✳

In a lifetime, most of us receive only a handful of gifts of true lasting value. Usually, these are handmade, or very carefully chosen. As I've already mentioned, I think the most original gifts can be made from discoveries from the junk shops. Nearly all of my close friends have one "Sari Original" in their dwellings. Each was designed to suit the receiver, but only after years of friendship gave me the necessary knowledge of their tastes.

On the other hand, a close friend of mine dropped by last week with a little old caboose stove in tow. She explained that she was driving past "this shop," and she saw "this thing" in the yard. She knew I would love it and she bought it.

And I do. I treasure that quaint little stove, and I've used it for many things. First, though, I sanded down the rust, and painted it with several coats of flat black.

We were having a luau, so I set the stove on the patio and filled it with charcoal briquettes. Our guests thought the giant hibachi was "groovy," as they broiled most un-Hawaiian Scottish Woodcocks over the coals.

You don't have to be Scottish (though I am) to enjoy this unusual Scottish hors d'oeuvres. If you're interested, you make it by wrapping hardboiled eggs in sausage meat that's been seasoned with salt, pepper and prepared mustard. Roll them in beaten egg and cracker crumbs and broil until the sausage is done. Eat by cutting into slices and dipping in tangy sauce.

75

My caboose stove as a planter.

As summer dwindled to an end, I used the little caboose stove in my living room as a planter. A clay pot fits right down inside and holds ferns. Maybe, someday, I'll turn it into a giant incense burner? Who knows.

✳✳✳✳✳✳✳✳✳✳✳✳✳✳✳✳✳✳✳✳✳✳✳✳✳✳

You say you have a sophisticate on your shopping list? You say that she is extremely hard to please? Well I suggest that you look in the junkshops for the heavy iron brackets that were used to bolt pews and railings to the floors of churches and courtrooms. Undoubtedly, they'll

The transformation of a pew bracket—removing rust, spraying with rust-preventative and then with paint. Voila! A unique candle holder.

be rusty. Soak them overnight in equal parts vinegar and water in a plastic container. Scrub with steel wool and let dry. Now spray with a base coat of rust preventative paint. Finish with two coats of your desired color. Set a decorative candle in the hole on top. Have you ever seen a more worldly-looking candleholder? By now, your gift is actually priceless. That's the best gift for a sophisticate.

✳✳✳✳✳✳✳✳✳✳✳✳✳✳✳✳✳✳✳✳✳✳✳✳✳

To me, my husband is sophisticated. His birthday was fast approaching and I wanted to give him something . . . priceless. He'd mentioned, frequently, that he wanted a bar. So I made one. A footlocker, stripped and refinished, became an excellent bar when opened, and a darling coffeetable when closed. Footlockers are easy to find and fairly reasonable in price.

But little did I realize how much work is involved in removing that old canvas coating from a footlocker. Ammonia, soap suds and a paint scraper did little to budge it. Then I brushed on a coat of furniture stripper. This loosened it. When it was rinsed, I set the children to pulling off the remnants of the canvas and cardboard. Incidentally, the wood beneath all this was beautiful pine.

For their work, the children each received a dime for a popsicle. A sanding with fine paper brightened the brass trimmings and smoothed the wood. Yet both retained an antique appearance. I rubbed black paste shoe polish, lightly, into the wood grain with steel wool. I sealed it with a heavy coat of hi-gloss varnish.

Now, the interior was my problem. I'd had it with stripping that old cloth off, and the inside was coated with it. So, I thought of lining it with fur. Yes, fur! I went to a material shop and bought a yard of fake leopard. I glued strips of leopard between the slats on top of the trunk, and I glued the rest to the interior of the trunk. I added utensils, glasses, napkins and the other items a good bartender needs.

To say that Don liked it is an understatement.

Don's footlocker bar.

Another fugitive from the trash can.

❉❉❉❉❉❉❉❉❉❉❉❉❉❉❉❉❉❉❉❉❉❉❉❉❉

I talk about quarters and dollars as though everyone has extra of these to spend. Some, I know, don't. Yet, they more than anyone else wish to add beauty to their lives by creating something attractive for their homes. May I suggest straw as an inexpensive material to create with.

I've often found baskets tossed in the trash. It's simple to cut strips of cardboard and reweave any broken parts. Spray paint, and these blend right in with the straw. One such basket I sprayed gold, adorned with pink roses, and filled with pink and green guest towels. It looks adorable sitting on the floor in the bathroom. To go with it, I found a smaller basket and decorated it to match. Here's where I put my fancy, scented guest soaps.

Baskets can be made into wastebaskets, magazine holders or picnic or sewing containers. Best of all, a natural-colored basket is the perfect foil for an armload of your own homemade paper flowers.

❉❉❉❉❉❉❉❉❉❉❉❉❉❉❉❉❉❉❉❉❉❉❉❉❉

Happiness is having two precious hours of time all to yourself.

11.

Cooking with Junk

THERE'S nothing I hate worse than housecleaning. And I'm just plain stupid at sewing. But I love to cook. In addition to constantly plying my husband with wild concoctions of food and drink, I like to do other things in the kitchen. In fact, our tiny kitchen is my at-home office and where I do most of my at-home coffee-klatching. And tiny it is, as are most modern kitchens. (Someday, I hope to have an old country kitchen with a brick floor, pantry and a fireplace.)

Meanwhile, to avoid a cluttered look, I keep all small appliances stored away. The toaster, for instance, is hidden in an antique tin breadbox. A shadowy, inaccessible corner beneath the overhanging cabinets was the perfect spot for this large, bright-orange accessory. Other touches of orange can be found in the wallpaper, shutters at the window, ceramic tile behind the built-in stove. To operate the toaster, you just lift a small portion of the lid and push a button down.

Mixer, blender and all other appliances are stored in cabinets. And only a few decorative canisters are left

My "expensive" copper and glass canisters.

on the cabinet top. (I need as much working space as I can get, because I'm one of those cooks who use every pot and pan in the kitchen.)

Each of my canisters was carefully picked to help set a country mood in an ultra-modern kitchen. No sterilized look for me, thank you. Two of the canisters were crocks from a junkshop. Though of different size, they're both gray trimmed with blue. If you're lucky enough to collect a complete set of crocks, you can have wooden lids made at a lumber yard for a minimal charge. I chanced to find the lids I needed at a garage sale.

Next to these are two elegant copper and glass lantern-type canisters that were very expensive . . . so I waited until they were put on sale. This may sound like a fish story, but I picked them up at a well-known florist-gift-shop at the end-of-the-year-damaged-goods-sale. One had a tiny screw missing; the other wouldn't unscrew. I fixed both with tweezers and patience. The one holds popcorn, the other looks charming filled with red chili peppers. (My dad sends me these from Albuquerque, and I use them liberally.)

I've mentioned rubbling, but did I tell you that men seem to enjoy it as much as women? Hanging on the wall above my canisters are several walnut carvings Don and I have found while rubbling through old homes. There's a bread and cheese board, a tray, and a daisy.

The tiny space next to the built-in oven holds an old pottery pitcher from Galena. Filled with pine boughs in the winter, ivy or cattails (preserved with glycerin and water) in the summer, it adds a touch of the outdoors.

Lucky as ever, I picked-up a vintage, labyrinth style vase at a housesale. Here's where I store real onions and potatoes. They contribute a quaint yet hardy, peasant look to my kitchen.

Periodically, dark, mysterious bean pots clutter my refrigerator in the summer. What do they hold? Fresh mushrooms marinating in lemon, oil and seasonings. And our children can't keep their grimy hands out of the crock that's steeping sliced cucumbers and onions in a secret german pickle juice. (Sorry, I promised I'd never give that recipe away.)

A labyrinth-style vase I picked up at a housesale.

As a lark, we tried our hand at camping . . . in a tent. Unfortunately, we were hooked. Unlike most campers, who buy a nice aluminum cooking set to carry along, I jaunted to the antique shop. Here, I picked-up a huge old spider frying pan and a dainty, lidded, cast-iron kettle. (The former, I was told, had belonged to a camping family for ten years. The latter, I know, is a collector's item, possibly from the pioneer days.) Anyway, the one is perfect for bacon and eggs, soups or zucchini. The other is my baked beans pot, and simmers on the back of the grill with zippy tomato sauce, brown sugar, mustard and onions.

When not on the campground, these antique kettles dot my stove and are in use in the kitchen. Incidentally, the first thing my mom gave me as a bride was a huge, five-quart dutch oven. A family heirloom, it's proved to be the most useful container in my kitchen. From here come my ragouts, stews, spaghetti sauce, homemade soups, chili, sloppy joes and just about everything that isn't broiled. A Frenchman once told me that every good French house-wife keeps a huge iron kettle simmering at the back of her stove. All edible leftovers are scraped into this, making those wonderful, hearty broths that the French are famous for.

"And," he whispered, "that's the secret to those marvelous French complexions."

Our circular kitchen table nestles between two gold-colored walls. Can you stand looking at a wall at 6:30 A.M. on a frosty, dreary morning? I can't, so I bought a lovely painting of the ocean (to me, it's Carmel-by-the-Sea), framed it and hung it on one of those walls. A-h-h-h, the view is breathtaking.

For many years now, it's been "out" to hang a single painting. If you go by the books, it's groupings or nothing. Bit by bit, I began to fill those two kitchen walls. Adding just enough, but not too much, was the challenge. Oh, sure, I enjoy walking through homes where everything's a collection and the texture of the decor is rich. But I can

My kitchen wall, including, among other things, the shoe hanger mentioned on page 17, and the old cloakroom hanger used to hang my collection of antique utensils on.

live on a rich diet so long, then I must reduce. Same for decor.

I added a horseshoe from a sheriff's office and ice tongs painted to match the horseshoe hold paper toweling. On another wall I hung a ceramic tray, painted curtain tie-backs, an ancient coffee grinder, my primitive kitchen utensil collection, a picture I painted of butterflies, and other oddities that catch everyone's eye because they're interesting in themselves.

85

Lastly, I've added several seashells to my kitchen decor
. . . just to remind me that life has a basic simple pattern
that rolls on and on, and will continue long after I'm gone.
Somehow this bolsters me. I feel at peace. That's why
there's a shell in every room in our house. . . .

✻✻✻✻✻✻✻✻✻✻✻✻✻✻✻✻✻✻✻✻✻✻✻✻✻

I wonder if any of you can guess what that charming
item in the picture is. I've heard it called many things—
slop bucket, chamber pot, thundermug. Everytime I show
this item at my programs, the audience giggles. So, I did
some research. I found that chamberpots were originally

A real kookie cookie jar.

My "flying duck" planter. I think you can tell what it was originally used for.

made so that after you'd washed your hands in a basin of water (pouring the water from a pitcher), you poured the dirty water into the thundermug, then tossed it out the back door. The other thing is another thing.

And I just chanced to find another "thing" hanging on the wall in an exclusive shop in Longgrove, Ill. Well, when I saw that charming, lemon-yellow "patio planter," I asked the dealer if it was imported Mexican pottery.

"No, deary," he shook his head disparagingly. "It's an antique flying duck."

I'd never seen a flying duck look like that, but I could see that mustard-yellow planter hanging on my patio fence, filled with geraniums, and I couldn't resist it. Could you?

As for "thundermugs," did you know they're selling for eighteen dollars and up? And being used for many things. A pair of artists I know turned their thundermug into a champagne bucket. They simply filled it with chipped ice, and shoved vintage wine down inside. It was the hit of the party.

An enterprising housewife uses her thundermug for a planter, a wastebasket, a diaper pail or a casserole, depending on her need that week. (Fortunately, I've never been invited to one of her macaroni-and-cheese casserole dinners, though several neighbors rave about her cooking. I daresay, they don't know much about antiques, or her active imagination.)

My favorite trick with a thundermug is to cleanse it well with ammonia, rinse and turn it into . . . a cookie jar, what else? (Or is it "kooky" jar?)

If you've wanted to become a collector, "a junkee," antiquer, or whatever you call it, may I suggest that you start this hobby with a collection of primitive kitchen utensils. They're easy to find, inexpensive, and practical as well as decorative. And if you travel—the islands, Europe, America—you can find primitive cooking utensils that will actually reflect the area you visited.

Once you've got a collection started, you'll need something to mount them on. May I recommend that you attend auctions, and comb your local antique shops for an old schoolroom coat hanger. These usually sell for between $3.50 and five dollars. (Once again I got a bargain. My cloakroom hanger cost two dollars because it was covered with chicken . . . feathers. Well, once I got it scoured and painted bright orange, it was a real "find.")

The first utensil I picked up was a potato masher. These are usually made of pine or maple and cost one dollar to five dollars, depending on size and shape. Remove any paint with a "stripper" and leave these "primitive" so they may be used in the kitchen, rinsed under the tap, and hung back on your cloakroom hanger. Uses? I find they're marvelous for crushing fresh strawberries, ice cubes, garlic and . . . when you go on the warpath.

While visiting my dad in New Mexico, I found a little chuckwagon frying pan. About four inches across, it was too small to do anything practical with. So I turned it into a picture frame for my Pillsbury Bake-Off prize-winning recipe—Hawaiian Tuna Puffs.

I simply cut the recipe from a magazine in an oval shape that would fit exactly in the bottom of the pan and glued it down. I added a ruffle of calico material, orange and red, and hung it next to my potato masher.

Many people are elaborating on this idea. They purchase a small, black-iron frying pan; paste in a bright background of wallpaper, burlap or other material; arrange miniature kitchen utensils and a recipe, and have a darling collage. Also a marvelous gift item.

In New York, I found a crumber set made of what looked like tarnished metal. When I tested it with my magnet it was repelled. I left the set to soak in a stripper overnight, and by morning I had genuine copper!

I think this is part of the thrill of "junkshopping." You pay a dollar for an item and it can turn out to be worth six. This doesn't happen often enough to make me a mililonaire, but enough so that I can't resist the lure of those wonderful, moldy-smelling shops.

In the past several years, many antique dealers have been moving their shops out to the suburbs. I'm sure this reflects the growing popularity of this hobby, and a new way of decorating in America. In and around our small suburb there are twelve shops, some existing only in basements, others in two and three buildings completely filled and overflowing into the yards.

In a newer shop, I found a darling little bristle brush with an ornate brass handle. (The brass was dirty, but repelled the magnet.) I asked what it was.

"That's an old stove brush," murmured the dealer. "Matter of fact, I think that one's from England. But 'cause ya got such a nice smile this mornin', ya can have it fer two dollars."

When I got home, I started cleaning the brass with ammonia. I found some letters engraved in the brass. I got my magnifying glass. Could it be the name of a long-dead owner? Perhaps a duke or something . . . the King of England!

And there it was. The writing said: Fuller Brush, Westfield, New Jersey. This can happen to anyone, as you might have discovered. You can't be too careful. Just ask me. I know.

I now had one hook left empty on my cloakroom hanger. And my mom filled it—by giving me an old onion chopper. Many people use their chopper every day, and I've become one of them. In fact, in 1961 I chopped up some onion and some celery. I sauteed them in a little butter, added a can of tuna, some pineapple chunks and a little horseradish. (Are you nauseated?) I whipped up a creampuff pastry, adding a teaspoon of soy sauce just to be different.

I baked the creampuffs the size of a quarter. When they'd cooled, I filled them with the tuna mixture. I served this recipe at a cocktail party and everyone just loved it. So, I entered it in a national cooking contest. About a month later, I received a phone call:

"Mrs. Kaysser, congratulations. You're a national cooking contest winner. We want to fly you to Beverly Hills for a week."

I was absolutely thrilled. But I told him I was sorry I couldn't go, I was 8½ months pregnant.

Several days before I was to leave, I changed my mind. I wanted to go. I wanted to bake my prize-winning recipe and maybe win thousands of dollars and an appearance on national television. My husband couldn't leave his high school students—no one could substitute for the three classes he taught. But I went anyway, alone on the train for three days and nights, And when I stepped off into beautiful sunny California, there was a band and a sign that read: WELCOME MAMA KAYSSER!

A charming gentleman handed me a bouquet of roses and the mayor kissed me on the cheek. What was the big deal? I was the first pregnant woman to attend this national cook-off. Isn't that a glamorous distinction?

I had a marvelous time touring Hollywood, baking and meeting celebrities. But my big moment finally came: They were televising the last day of the cook-off and I'd already called Don and asked him to bring a portable TV to his classroom. Just in case.

When they dollied those big cameras into my little kitchen, I couldn't believe it. I was one of the ten chosen, from over a hundred, that they would televise!

A dapper gentleman stepped over to me. And he said: "Good morning, Mrs. Kaysser." He chuckled, winked and said, "What's cooking in the oven today, Mama Kaysser?"

Well, my husband's class started laughing, and eventually he quit teaching because they teased him so much. Eventually, he became a salesman for computers, which worked out better anyway. But I had a marvelous time, plus I came home with prizes and wonderful memories.

All it takes is one original recipe, one that uses flour, sugar or what have you and you can win big prizes. And several of the past winners told me that they found their winning recipes in antique cookbooks.

Antique cookbooks are very "in" right now, as are old medical books. One of my favorites, *The Everyday Cookbook*, published in 1890, contains the recipes for drying flowers and preserving vines.

✷✷✷✷✷✷✷✷✷✷✷✷✷✷✷✷✷✷✷✷✷✷✷✷✷

A piece of junk in your hand is worth two in your attic.

12.

Paper Hands I Love...

"COLLAGE" is a word in common use today. My own interpretation is that it means any number or types of three-dimensional or flat objects arranged together on any background you choose, in a frame or not. A collage emphasizes symbolism, color, texture and design.

Several years ago, an expert in Chicago's Old Town, showed me how to make a collage.

He said: "Just throw five things in a frame and sell it for fifty dollars and up."

Well, I think you ought to begin your "Kitchen Collage" with a pie-shell-type picture frame. The deeper the sides of the frame, the more expensive it is. And these make good investments because they're usually quite old and keep going up on the market.

Strip your pie-shell frame (if it needs it) and, instead of refinishing with stain and shellac, or whatever method you've previously used, try my secret method: Use paste shoe polish. Rub the polish into the raw wood with fine steel wool. Let it dry. Apply a second coat, if you wish

My kitchen collage.

a darker stain. This gives a natural-looking semi-gloss finish, makes a tough, protective coating when it's dry, and can be touched up easily if it gets scratched. Use brown paste polish for walnut and oak, tan boot polish on pine and maple.

Now select a colorful backing for your frame—wallpaper, contact, burlap or, as I did, a red farmer's handkerchief. Glue it down, smoothly, on the backing and insert the backing back into the refinished frame.

Again, go into the junk shop, this time seeking small, hand-carved kitchen utensils, hand-cut and soldered cookie cutters or whatever your imagination lights on. I found a darling hand-made knife, fork and spoon set of wood. I had it appraised and was delighted I'd paid just two dollars for a 102-year-old antique. I glued these in an interesting pattern on my handkerchief backing. Next, I glued down my blue cook-off ribbon. But may I suggest that you either bake a gingerbread cookie man or buy one in the bakery, unless you have a ribbon, too. Spray the cookie with plastic preservative. Let it dry, and spray again. You'll be delighted at how it will look when glued on your collage. And the cookie won't deteriorate. I know. I've made our Christmas ornaments this way for years. Eventually they get so hard that you could throw them right through the wall.

****

Let me tell you about my favorite creation: my hands picture. It all started when a Chicago newspaper asked me to do another article for them. This time, they wanted a story, a long story with plenty of photos, for their Sunday magazine section. It was to be about Maxwell Street, Chicago's equivalent of a European open-air flea market. Again, I was nearing the end of a pregnancy (my third), and I was hesitant . . . for about two seconds. Who could resist exploring that marvelous Maxwell bargain street at 6:30 A.M.? (You have to get there that early on Sunday to beat the antique dealers.)

You haven't lived until you've shared coffee and a bagel with the colorful inhabitants of early-morning Maxwell in the frost of February. You haven't seen bargains anywhere for such low prices, except maybe at European flea markets. Treasures are arranged on blankets, tables or just on the ground. And I found a marvelous solid oak picture frame for just a quarter. I gave it the paste-shoe-polish treatment.

About this time, Don came bounding home from work thrilled because he'd won a trip to Florida for being one of the top salesmen at his company. I was invited, too.

I asked when we were to go. He told me. Unfortunately, it was the same day our baby was due to be born. I told him to go ahead without me, but he said we'd wait, and go later in the year.

I wanted to do something special to show him how much I appreciated this. That frame, I vowed, would become an heirloom that he could hang in his office or the den; something that would show how much I cared; something he'd be proud of.

A family portrait was my first thought, a photo I'd mount in that frame. But we have plenty of those and I wanted something really different. Then it hit me, as I sat on the sofa watching Don playing with our two children at the dining room table. He was teaching them to outline their hands and his with paper and pencil. And I knew just what I'd do with those scraps the next day.

I'm certain you've all played this game with your children or your grandchildren. And you've probably tossed the paper into the garbage just as Don did.

The next morning when he'd gone off to work, I fished the papers out. I smoothed them and started to oil paint in colors of turquoise, gold and orange.

Unfortunately, I had to stop. (I can't stand to quit working right in the middle of a project, but I had no choice. The labor pains were two minutes apart.)

So I hauled out my suitcase and threw in robe, slippers, toothpaste, linseed oil, oil paints, old rags, glue, scissors, turpentine, brushes and all the things one needs in the hospital. I drove myself to the hospital and had our baby Tamma. (Of course, I called Don, too.)

They put me in a ward with two other girls, and I arranged my art supplies on the bed to finish my project. Believe me, those gals looked at me like I belonged in a ward—the kind with lock and key!

But I didn't let that bother me. When they brought the baby to me, I traced her tiny little hand right on the paper. Now the five hands were arranged with Don's at the top, mine right beneath his, then Terra's, Troy's and

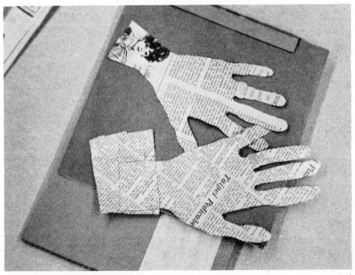

Tamma's. We were all reaching for something . . . beautiful.

The painting was striking, in my opinion, but for one thing: The background around the hands needed to be toned down, antiqued, so the hands would stand out three-dimensionally. But I'd forgotten to bring my antique-color paint. So I pulled a candle from my suitcase. (I always carry candles, don't you?) Anchoring the candle in an ashtray, I lit it and held the collage right over the flame. And this is how I discovered that antiquing with smoke is terrific. You'll like it because you can achieve many unique effects. And you seal the smoke with spray-on plastic preservative.

Don loved this picture, and it's been featured in several newspaper articles. Each year it seems to grow in value, as those little hands get larger.

✢✢✢✢✢✢✢✢✢✢✢✢✢✢✢✢✢✢✢✢✢✢✢

I wish you all "Happy Junkshopping" and I hope that you agree with me by now that: "IT'S NOT REALLY JUNK. IT'S JUST SOMETHING THAT NEEDS AN IDEA.

Right?